The Children's Illustrated
ACTIVITY ATLAS

NEIL MORRIS

Gareth Stevens Children's Books
MILWAUKEE

For a free color catalog describing Gareth Stevens' list of high-quality children's books call 1 (800) 433-0942

Library of Congress Cataloging-in-Publication Data
Morris, Neil.
  The children's illustrated activity atlas.

  Includes index.
  Summary: Maps, activities, and text introduce regions and countries of the world and provide the opportunity to
practice the reading of maps and the interpretation of atlas symbols.
  1. Atlases. [1. Atlases. 2. Maps] I. Title. II. Title: Activity atlas.
G1021.M67   1989   912   88-42913
ISBN 1-55532-927-6

North American edition first published in 1989 by
Gareth Stevens Children's Books
7317 West Green Tree Road
Milwaukee, Wisconsin 53223, USA

Project editor: Neil Champion
Editor (US): Mark Sachner
Research editor (US): Scott Enk

Printed in the United States of America
1 2 3 4 5 6 7 8 9 95 94 93 92 91 90 89

CONTENTS

What is a map?

A map is an accurately drawn picture of the things around us on the Earth's surface. Maps are very useful because they show you the shape of the land, help you find out how far it is from one place to another, and show you how to get there.

Some maps only show a very small part of Earth. This may be your school or the city or village where you live. Other maps show entire regions, countries, or continents.

A globe shows Earth's shape as it really is. But a map must change this round shape so we can flatten it out.

1

2

3

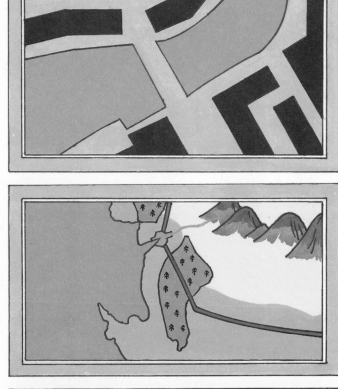

Map 1 is a close-up of map 2, showing the area around the bridge in detail. Map 3 uses a much smaller scale. In the same area on the page, it shows the entire island.

Maps show water and dry land, high mountains and low plains, on sheets of flat paper. It is not very easy to do this. A whole town, country, or even the world must fit onto a sheet of paper. This is done by using scale (see page 8).

The world is shaped like a ball. It is impossible to see all of the ball from one view. To see it all, we must flatten it out first (see page 5).

Also, because things on Earth's surface have been made smaller (using scale), they cannot be shown as they really are. So people who make maps use symbols (see page 9). Symbols are simple shapes and colors that stand for something in the real world, such as a capital city, a mountain range, an apple farm, or your school.

Making the Earth flat

The whole surface of a ball cannot be shown on a flat sheet of paper without cutting and stretching the ball. This is what we have to do to show the surface of Earth as a map.

If we pretend that Earth is an orange, we can divide it into segments. Even though the segments are not flat, we can now see the whole surface of the orange at once if we lay the segments out. Before we cut the orange, let's put a sticky label around it. This label will help us understand how a round shape becomes distorted when it is flattened out.

We could lay the segments in another pattern, like this:

Or we could arrange to have a special sticky label made in this shape:

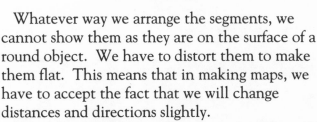

Whatever way we arrange the segments, we cannot show them as they are on the surface of a round object. We have to distort them to make them flat. This means that in making maps, we have to accept the fact that we will change distances and directions slightly.

The following pictures show how the shape of Australia can be changed by stretching it flat in different ways. Compare these maps with the map of Australia on page 41. The different ways of stretching are called projections.

Look what has happened to the label. To get rid of the cuts or gaps, and to bring the cut parts back together, we have to stretch the pieces so they touch one another, like this:

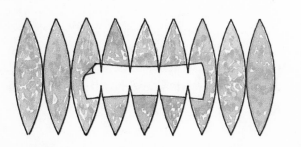

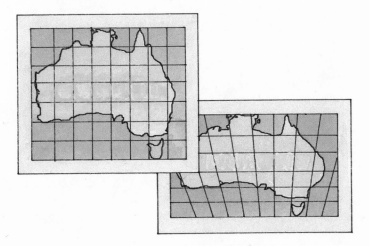

Finding the direction

Maps have a language you can learn. Their language begins with the four basic directions: north, south, east, and west. These directions answer the question, "Which way?"

North is the direction toward the North Pole from any place on Earth. South is toward the South Pole, in the opposite direction. As we face north, the direction to the right is called east. This is where the Sun appears every morning. The direction to the left as we face north is called west.

North is usually at the top of a map. If we want to find out which direction north is, we use a compass. The needle of the compass always points to north. And once we know which direction north is, we can figure out the other directions.

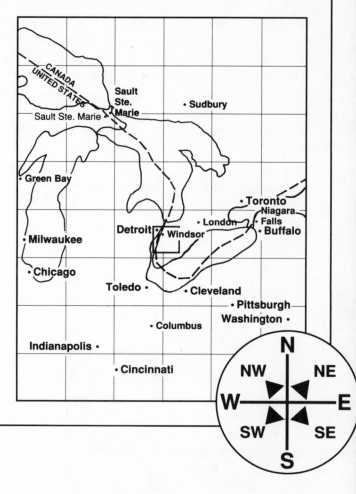

This map shows how we can use the points of a compass to divide up the continent of Africa.

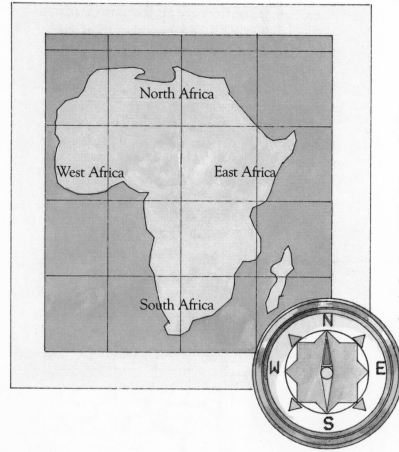

Using a compass, can you figure out in which direction you must travel from Detroit or Windsor to get to the other places marked on the map?

We can also describe other directions, too. Halfway between north and east is a direction called northeast. Halfway between east and south is called southeast.

Direction and distance can be used to describe the position of a place. For example, you could describe a city as being 100 miles (160 km) east of where you are. But we can also divide up areas, countries, and continents according to their compass position. For example, we talk about South Africa, which is a country in Africa, or East Africa, West Africa, and North Africa, which are regions that are made up of many countries.

Knowing where we are

Every place in the world has a particular position where it can always be found. You can find buildings and people by using their addresses. You have an address where letters are delivered. But what is the "address" of a city, a mountain, a forest, or an entire country?

Look at the picture below. It shows a city, a mountain, and a forest. It also has a grid of lines on it with numbers and letters down the side and along the top. Using these lines, we can give each of these places an address of sorts: The city is at A2, the mountain peak at B1, and the forest at C3. You can find the addresses by following the lines to their numbers and letters and putting them together.

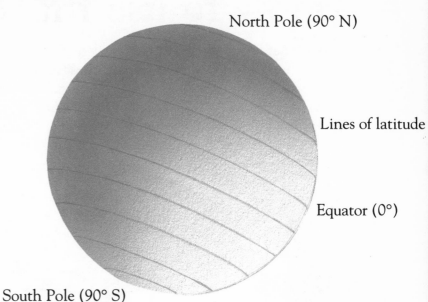

North Pole (90° N)

Lines of latitude

Equator (0°)

South Pole (90° S)

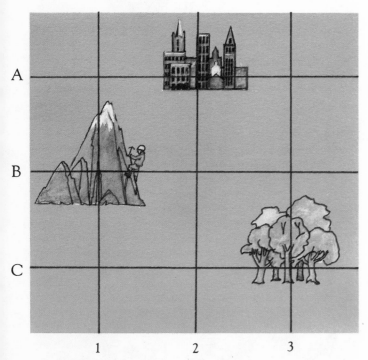

Lines of longitude are imaginary lines running up and down from the North Pole to the South Pole. They measure how far east or west a place is from a point known as the Greenwich meridian in London, England. This point is longitude zero. Lines of longitude are measured up to 180° east and 180° west. They meet on the other side of the world from Greenwich, near New Zealand.

Maps use imaginary lines called lines of latitude and longitude to divide the world. Lines of latitude are circles that are drawn around the globe. They measure how far north or south a place is. All the lines of latitude run parallel to the Equator. They are given a number (a degree, or °) north or south of the Equator. They reach a maximum of 90° north at the North Pole and 90° south at the South Pole.

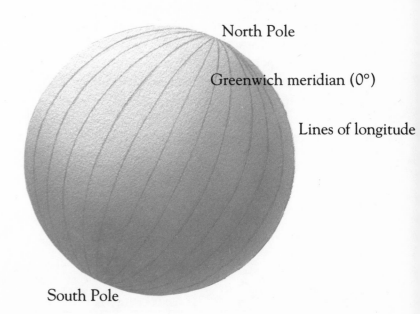

North Pole

Greenwich meridian (0°)

Lines of longitude

South Pole

How to use the scale bar

A toy car's scale is the difference in size between it and the real thing. Our toy is 32 inches (about 80 cm) long, and the real car on which it is based is 160 inches (400 cm) long. This means that 1 inch on the toy equals 5 inches on the real car. So the toy has a scale of 1:5. The real car is 5 times bigger than the toy.

A map scale is used in the same way. A scale of 1:1,000 means that if you measure a distance of 1 inch on the map, it would actually be 1,000 inches on the real ground. So scale is the system that brings things down to sizes that fit on paper. Scale lets you hold thousands of square miles on a map in your hand.

To make things easier, maps usually have a scale bar, where the measured distance and the real ground distance are matched to each other.

On each map in this atlas, the scale bar is shown as a ruler. One side shows centimeters and kilometers, and the other side shows inches and miles. The scale varies from map to map, so be careful when you measure with it!

You can measure distances on your maps by using paper. Put the edge of the paper along a line running between two points on the map. Put a mark by each point. Then put the paper on the scale bar and read off the real distance between the two points in miles or kilometers.

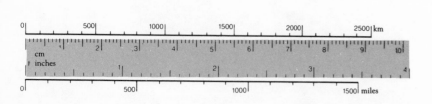

How to use the symbols

All maps use symbols. Symbols are simple images that stand for something more complicated in the real world. For example, if we want to show an area where cotton grows, we can show it by using a symbol like the one in the picture on the right. We know what a real cotton field looks like, so we can imagine it when we see the symbol on the map. But first we need to know what the symbols stand for. We can guess the meaning of some. Others may be more difficult.

Different maps use different kinds of symbols. The maps in this atlas use only a few symbols to show you some of the interesting things that go on in the world. But the world is a very complicated place, and there are many other products or activities that are not shown using our symbols.

Here are the symbols used in this atlas and their meaning, along with the meaning of the differently colored landscapes:

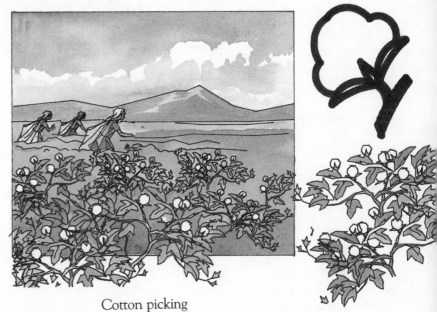

Cotton symbol

Cotton picking

- ⚓ **Major port**
- ✈ **International airport**
- 🐟 **Fishing zone**
- 🌾 **Cereal farming**
- 🍇 **Vineyards (Grapes)**
- 🌱 **Cotton fields**
- 🌿 **Sugar plantations**
- ✱ **Cattle farming**
- 🐑 **Sheep farming**
- 🐐 **Goat herding**
- **Rubber plantations**

- 🛒 **Coal mining**
- 🛢 **Oil wells**
- 🔥 **Gas**
- **Dam**
- ⚙ **Heavy industry**
- 🐘 **Game reserve**
- ■ **Capital city**
- □ **Important town or city**
- △ **Mountain peak**
- **Mountains**
- **Forest and scrub**
- **Desert**
- **Arable land**
- **Frozen desert (snow and ice)**

A R C T I C

GREENLAND
(Denmark)

U. S. S. R.

ALASKA
(U.S.A.)

CANADA

A
T
L
A
N
T
I
C

UNITED STATES
OF AMERICA

Tropic of Cancer

HAWAIIAN
ISLANDS (USA)

THE BAHAMAS

CUBA   HAITI   Puerto Rico (U.S.A.)
                DOMINICAN
                REP.   CAPE
MEXICO   JAMAICA   ANTIGUA AND BARBUDA   VERDE
                BELIZE   DOMINICA   ISLAND
                           ST. LUCIA
P A C I F I C   GUATEMALA HONDURAS ST. VINCENT
                EL SALVADOR   BARBADOS
                    NICARAGUA GRENADA
                              TRINIDAD AND TOBAGO
                COSTA RICA   VENEZUELA
                       PANAMA
                           COLOMBIA
Equator   FRENCH GUIANA
NAURU   O C E A N   GALÁPAGOS   ECUADOR   SURINAM
                           ISLANDS   GUYANA
PAPUA   K I R I B A T I (ECUADOR)
NEW   SOLOMON
GUINEA   ISLANDS   P
        TUVALU   E   B R A Z I L
                                                   R
VANUATU   U
     FIJI   WESTERN
                 SAMOA
                        TAHITI   BOLIVIA
         TONGA
Tropic of Capricorn   PARAGUAY
                 PITCAIRN Is.
                 (U.K.)   EASTER Is.   C
AUSTRALIA   (CHILE)   H
                                                   I
                                                   L   URUGUAY
                                                   E
                                              ARGENTINA
     NEW ZEALAND

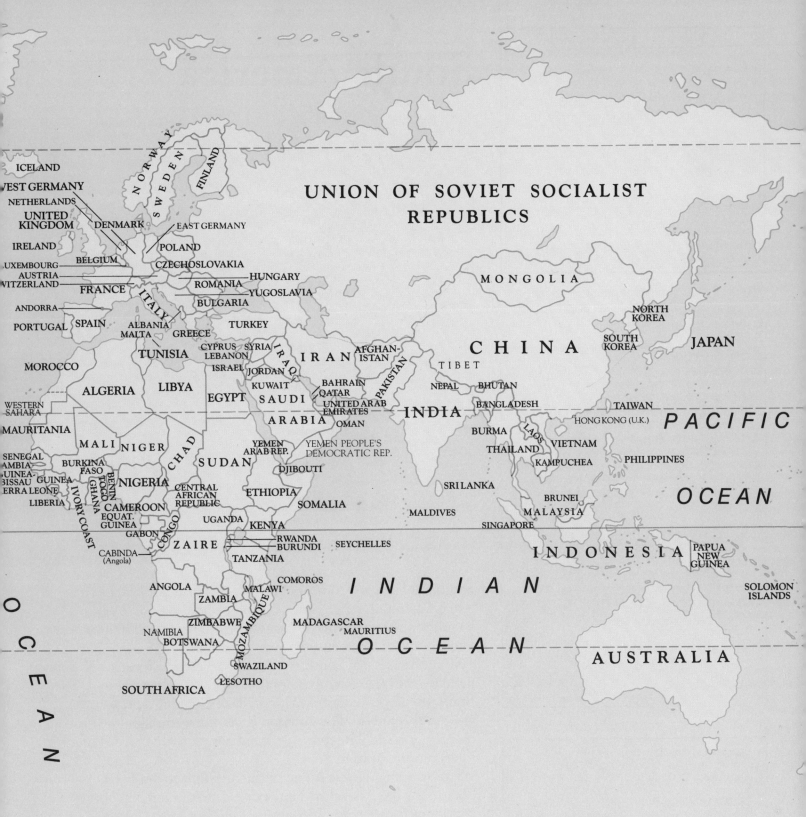

OCEAN

ICELAND
WEST GERMANY
NETHERLANDS
UNITED
KINGDOM   DENMARK   EAST GERMANY
IRELAND   POLAND
LUXEMBOURG   BELGIUM   CZECHOSLOVAKIA
AUSTRIA   HUNGARY
SWITZERLAND   FRANCE   ROMANIA   YUGOSLAVIA
                                       BULGARIA
ANDORRA
PORTUGAL   SPAIN   TURKEY
               ALBANIA   GREECE
               MALTA
           TUNISIA   CYPRUS   SYRIA
                               LEBANON
MOROCCO   ISRAEL   IRAQ   IRAN   AFGHAN-
                                       JORDAN   ISTAN
       ALGERIA   LIBYA   EGYPT   KUWAIT
WESTERN   SAUDI   BAHRAIN   PAKISTAN
SAHARA   QATAR
MAURITANIA   ARABIA   UNITED ARAB
                                       EMIRATES   OMAN
               MALI   NIGER   YEMEN   YEMEN PEOPLE'S
SENEGAL   CHAD   ARAB REP.   DEMOCRATIC REP.
GAMBIA   BURKINA   SUDAN
GUINEA-   FASO   DJIBOUTI
BISSAU   GUINEA
SIERRA LEONE   NIGERIA
LIBERIA   GHANA   CENTRAL   ETHIOPIA
       IVORY COAST   BENIN   AFRICAN
               TOGO   CAMEROON   REPUBLIC
               EQUAT.   SOMALIA
               GUINEA
           GABON   CONGO   UGANDA   KENYA
CABINDA   ZAIRE   RWANDA
(Angola)   BURUNDI   SEYCHELLES
                               TANZANIA
       ANGOLA   COMOROS
               ZAMBIA   MALAWI
               ZIMBABWE   MADAGASCAR
NAMIBIA   MOZAMBIQUE   MAURITIUS
       BOTSWANA

UNION OF SOVIET SOCIALIST
REPUBLICS

MONGOLIA

NORTH
KOREA
CHINA   SOUTH
               KOREA   JAPAN
TIBET
NEPAL   BHUTAN
       BANGLADESH   TAIWAN
INDIA   HONG KONG (U.K.)   PACIFIC
BURMA   VIETNAM
       LAOS
THAILAND
       KAMPUCHEA   PHILIPPINES
SRI LANKA   OCEAN
               BRUNEI
MALDIVES   MALAYSIA
SINGAPORE

INDONESIA   PAPUA
                   NEW
                   GUINEA
                               SOLOMON
                               ISLANDS

INDIAN

SWAZILAND
LESOTHO

OCEAN   AUSTRALIA

SOUTH AFRICA

OCEAN

ANTARCTICA

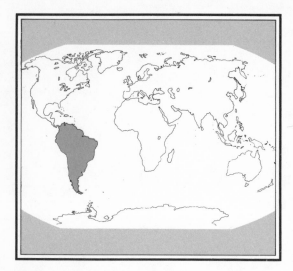

South America

Activities

- How far is it from Brasília to Buenos Aires?

- Which is the largest country in South America?

- The Equator runs through three South American countries. Which are they?

- Which six countries lie on longitude 60° W? And which islands?

- In which ocean is the mouth of the Amazon River?

- What is the capital of Venezuela?

- Mount Chimborazo is an extinct volcano in the Andes. How high is it?

- How many countries are there in South America?

Regional Facts

Population: 270 million

Largest Country: Brazil

Smallest Country: French Guiana

Largest City: São Paulo, Brazil, 7 million people

Highest Mountain: Aconcagua, Argentina, 22,831 ft (6,959 m)

Longest River: Amazon, 4,000 miles (6,440 km) — the second longest river in the world

South America is a continent of very different landscapes. The Andes mountain range runs near the Pacific coast along the length of the continent. It is nearly 4,500 miles (7,250 km) long. Some of the mountains are volcanoes.

More than half of South America is covered by forests. This includes the huge Amazonian rain forest, found mainly in Brazil, the largest country. Hundreds of different types of trees grow in this forest. The Amazon River flows through it. It is one of the world's greatest rivers and has more than 1,000 small rivers running into it.

The Atacama Desert is one of the driest places on Earth. Some parts have never had any rain. The southern tip of the continent is very cold. It is not far from the harsh, frozen wastes of Antarctica.

The first people to live in South America were tribal Indians. About 400 years ago, Spanish and Portuguese people landed and started to colonize different areas. Today, most of the people in the continent's thirteen countries speak either Spanish or Portuguese. Indian languages are spoken in some parts. Most people practice the Roman Catholic religion, brought over from Europe.

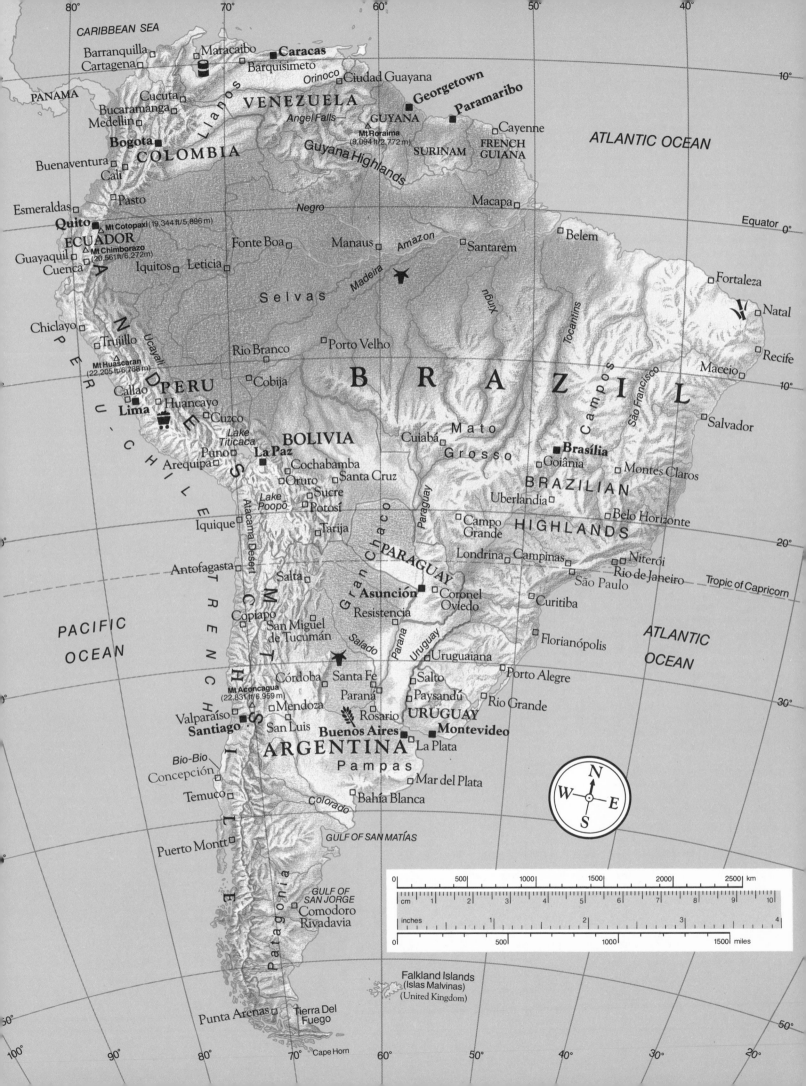

CARIBBEAN SEA

80° 70° 60° 50° 40°

PANAMA

Barranquilla
Cartagena
Maracaibo
Caracas
Barquisimeto
Orinoco
Ciudad Guayana
10°
Georgetown
Paramaribo
Cucuta
VENEZUELA
Angel Falls
GUYANA
Cayenne
Bucaramanga
Llanos
Mt Roraima
(9,094 ft/2,772 m)
SURINAM
FRENCH
GUIANA
ATLANTIC OCEAN
Medellin
Bogota
COLOMBIA
Guyana Highlands
Buenaventura
Cali
Pasto
Macapa
Esmeraldas
Negro
Equator 0°
Quito
Mt Cotopaxi (19,344 ft/5,896 m)
Belem
ECUADOR
Fonte Boa
Manaus
Amazon
Santarem
Mt Chimborazo
(20,561ft/6,272 m)
Guayaquil
Iquitos
Leticia
Fortaleza
Cuenca
Selvas
Madeira
Natal
Chiclayo
Xingu
Trujillo
Ucayali
Rio Branco
Porto Velho
Tocantins
Recife
Mt Huascaran
(22,205 ft/6,768 m)
Cobija
B R A Z I L
Maceio
Callao
PERU
São Francisco
10°
Huancayo
Salvador
Lima
Cuzco
Lake
Titicaca
BOLIVIA
Cuiabá
Mato
Grosso
Brasília
Puno
Arequipa
La Paz
Cochabamba
Goiânia
Montes Claros
Oruro
Santa Cruz
BRAZILIAN
Sucre
Lake
Poopó
Potosí
Uberlandia
Belo Horizonte
Iquique
Tarija
Paraguay
Campo
Grande
HIGHLANDS
Atacama Desert
Gran Chaco
PARAGUAY
Londrina
Campinas
Niterói 20°
Antofagasta
Salta
Rio de Janeiro
Tropic of Capricorn
Asunción
Coronel
Oviedo
São Paulo
Copiapo
Resistencia
Curitiba
San Miguel
de Tucumán
Salado
Parana
Uruguay
Florianópolis
PACIFIC
Uruguaiana
ATLANTIC
OCEAN
Córdoba
Santa Fe
Salto
OCEAN
Mt Aconcagua
(22,831 ft/6,959 m)
Parana
Paysandú
Porto Alegre
Valparaíso
Mendoza
Rosario
Rio Grande 30°
Santiago
San Luis
URUGUAY
Buenos Aires
Montevideo
Bio-Bio
La Plata
Concepción
ARGENTINA
Pampas
Temuco
Mar del Plata
Colorado
Bahía Blanca

N
W E
S

Puerto Montt
GULF OF SAN MATÍAS

Patagonia

GULF OF
SAN JORGE
Comodoro
Rivadavia

| 0 | 500 | 1000 | 1500 | 2000 | 2500 | km |

| cm | 1 | 2 | 3 | 4 | 5 | 6 | 7 | 8 | 9 | 10 |

| inches | 1 | 2 | 3 | 4 |

| 0 | 500 | 1000 | 1500 | miles |

Punta Arenas
Tierra Del
Fuego

Falkland Islands
(Islas Malvinas)
(United Kingdom)

Cape Horn

Central America, Mexico, and the Caribbean

Working on a sugar plantation.

Actually part of North America, Mexico is the largest country in this region. It is almost four times bigger than the seven countries of Central America put together. At the southern end of Central America, the Caribbean Sea is joined to the Pacific Ocean by the Panama Canal.

Most of the people of this area are a mixture of Indians who first lived here and Europeans who came to find gold. More than half are mestizos, a mixture of American Indian and European ancestry. The European colonizers brought in Christianity, but in some areas traditional Indian religions are still practiced.

In the Caribbean Sea there is a group of islands that stretches in a crescent shape from Florida to Venezuela in South America. Cuba is the largest island, and nearly half of all Caribbean island people live in Cuba and Haiti.

The people of the Caribbean come from many different ethnic backgrounds. Many are descended from slaves brought from Africa to work on sugar plantations. The islands have a warm, tropical climate that is very popular with vacationers from other countries. Most people work on farms or in hotels, shops, and small factories. Fruit, sugar cane, cotton, and coffee are grown, and much is sold to other countries.

Regional Facts

Population: 110 million

Largest Country: Mexico

Smallest Country: Bermuda

Largest City: Mexico City, Mexico, 14 million people

Highest Mountain: Citlaltepetl, Mexico, 18,701 ft (5,700 m)

Longest River: Rio Grande, 1,760 miles (2,832 km)

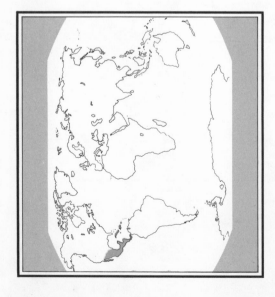

Activities

- What is the capital of Honduras?
- How far is it from Tijuana to Monterrey?
- How many countries are there in Central America?
- In which direction do you travel from Monterrey to Mexico City?
- Which island is the largest in the Caribbean Sea?
- Which Central American country lies on latitude 10° N?
- Which ocean is to the north of the West Indies?
- Which four countries border on Guatemala?
- Which republic shares an island with Haiti?
- How high is the highest mountain in Guatemala?

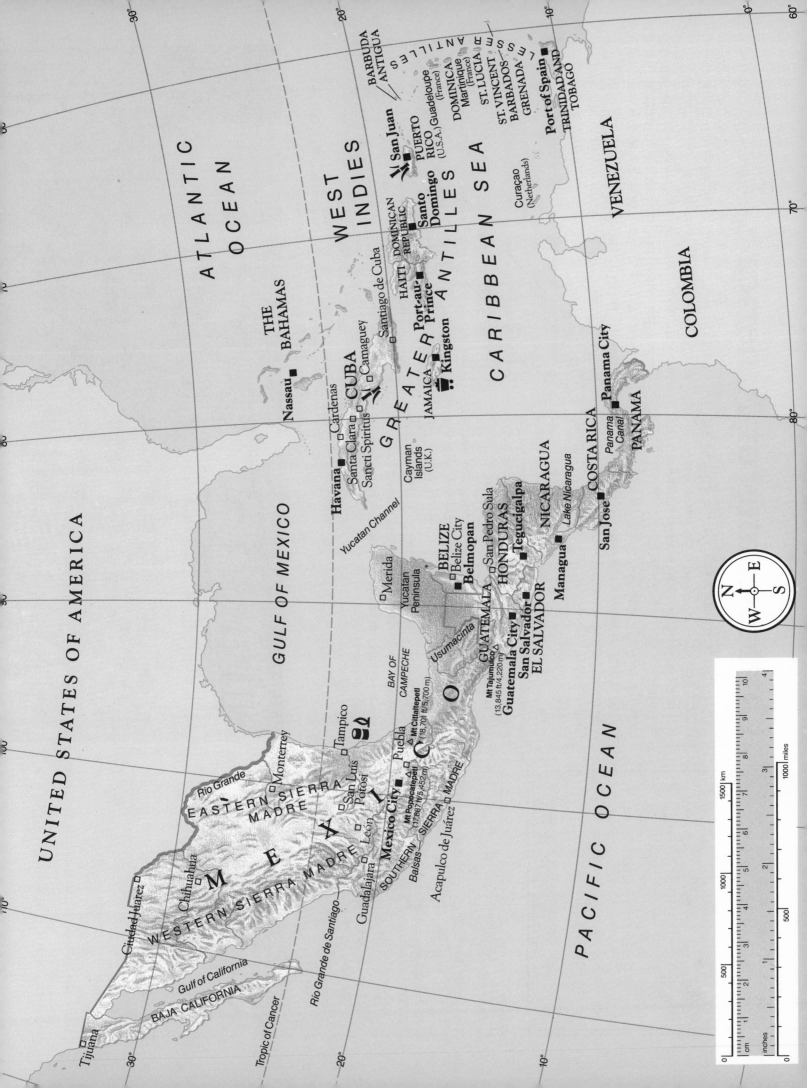

UNITED STATES OF AMERICA

ATLANTIC OCEAN

WEST INDIES

THE BAHAMAS

Nassau

Cardenas

Havana
Santa Clara
Sancti Spiritus

CUBA

Camaguey

Santiago de Cuba

GREATER

San Juan

PUERTO RICO (U.S.A.)

Guadeloupe (France)

BARBUDA
ANTIGUA

DOMINICA
Martinique (France)

ST. LUCIA
ST. VINCENT
BARBADOS
GRENADA

Port of Spain
TRINIDAD AND TOBAGO

DOMINICAN REPUBLIC

HAITI
Port-au-Prince

Santo Domingo

ANTILLES

Curaçao (Netherlands)

VENEZUELA

COLOMBIA

CARIBBEAN SEA

Kingston
JAMAICA

Cayman Islands (U.K.)

Yucatan Channel

GULF OF MEXICO

Merida

Yucatan Peninsula

BELIZE
Belize City
Belmopan

San Pedro Sula

GUATEMALA

Usumacinta

Mt Tajumulco
(13,845 ft/4,220 m)

Guatemala City

San Salvador
EL SALVADOR

HONDURAS
Tegucigalpa

NICARAGUA

Managua

Lake Nicaragua

COSTA RICA

San Jose

Panama Canal

Panama City

PANAMA

Tampico

BAY OF CAMPECHE

Mt Citlaltepetl
(18,701 ft/5,700 m)

Monterrey

Rio Grande

San Luis Potosi

Puebla
Mexico City

Mt Popocatepetl
(17,887 ft/5,452 m)

MEXICO

Leon

Guadalajara

SOUTHERN

Balsas

SIERRA MADRE

Acapulco de Juárez

Chihuahua

EASTERN SIERRA MADRE

WESTERN SIERRA MADRE

Gulf of California

BAJA CALIFORNIA

Ciudad Juárez

Tijuana

Rio Grande de Santiago

Tropic of Cancer

PACIFIC OCEAN

N
E
S
W

1500 km
1000
500
0

1000 miles
500
0

cm   inches

United States of America (lower forty-eight states)

The United States of America is one of the largest, richest, and most powerful countries in the world. It is made up of fifty states, several territories, and Washington, D. C. From 1912 until 1959, its flag carried forty-eight stars (one for each of the states) and thirteen stripes (for the original thirteen colonies). In January 1959, Alaska joined the United States to become the biggest state, followed by Hawaii in August 1959.

The first Europeans came to settle what is now the U.S. almost 400 years ago. They came from England and settled what became New England and Jamestown, Virginia. Others came from places like Spain and Holland, naming the places they settled after the places they had left behind. But people were already living in this land before the Europeans came. The Europeans called them Indians. There were many battles among Indians and Europeans, until the Europeans controlled almost all the land.

The U.S. is a mixture of cultures from many different nations. This has given the country a rich variety of lifestyles, food, music, and art. These have come from Indians, black Africans (brought to the U.S. as slaves), Europeans (such as Spanish, British, Dutch, Irish, Italian, and Slavic peoples), Asians, Latin Americans, and others.

Country Facts

Population: 244 million

Capital: Washington, D. C., 3 million people

Largest City: New York, 9 million people

Highest Mountain: McKinley, Alaska, 20,320 ft (6,194 m) (see pages 18 and 19)

Longest River: Missouri, 3,710 miles (5,969 km)

The U.S. is the fourth largest country in the world.

City children play baseball, a sport known as the "national pastime" by many in the United States.

Activities

- How far is it by direct flight from New Orleans to Miami?

- The smallest state lies between Massachusetts and Connecticut. What is it?

- Which ocean is to the west of the mainland United States?

- Which state is just to the east of Arizona?

- What is the highest mountain in the lower forty-eight states and what famous city is it close to?

- What is the capital of the U.S.?

- In which state is the Grand Canyon?

- On what river is the Hoover Dam?

- What are the main mountain ranges in the lower forty-eight states?

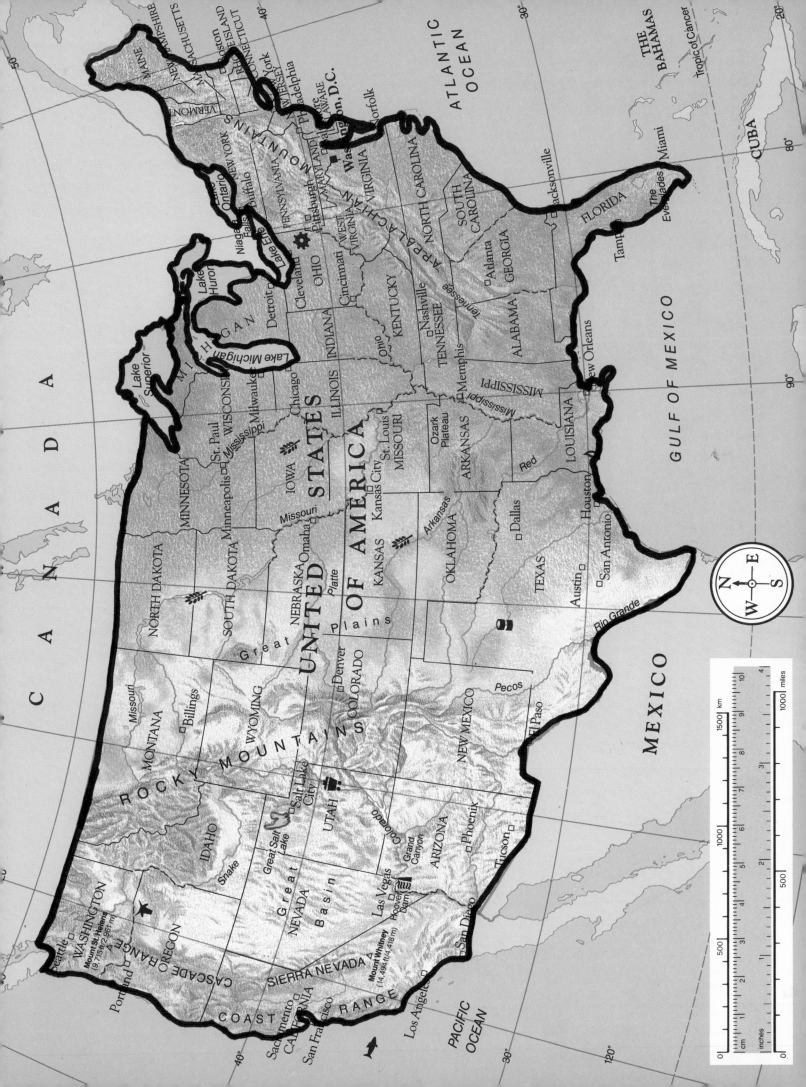

Canada, Alaska (U.S.), and Greenland

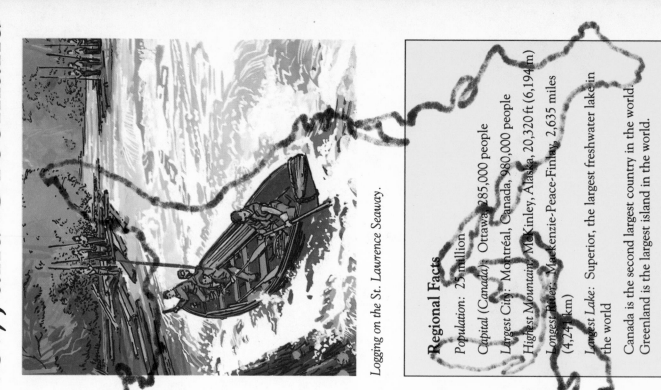

Canada is the second largest country in the world after the U.S.S.R. Much of Canada is very cold in winter and covered with snow. In the north is a group of large, ice-covered islands in the Arctic Ocean, where very few people live.

South of the islands are vast areas of pine forest. Most Canadians live in the country's southernmost part, near the Great Lakes and the St. Lawrence River. Part of the Canada-U.S. border runs through the lakes and the river.

To the northwest of the Great Lakes are Canada's prairies, where enormous wheat farms stretch as far as the eye can see. Farther west are the high Rocky Mountains, which stretch down into the United States.

Most of the Canadian people are of British and French descent. American Indians and Inuit (Eskimo) were the original inhabitants.

Canada is one of the world's richest countries. Wheat farming, wood, fish, oil, minerals, and gas provide great wealth for this modern nation.

Alaska is joined to Canada but is a part of the U.S. It is the largest of the states in area, but because it is mostly frozen, mountainous, and barren, few people live there.

Greenland is nearly covered by a huge ice cap, making it the world's largest ice mass outside of Antarctica. Because of its extreme climate and geography, only about 54,000 people live in Greenland, most of them a mixture of native Inuit and mainly Danish European immigrants.

Logging on the St. Lawrence Seaway.

Regional Facts

Population: 25 million

Capital (Canada): Ottawa, 285,000 people

Largest City: Montréal, Canada, 980,000 people

Highest Mountain: McKinley, Alaska, 20,320 ft (6,194m)

Longest River: Mackenzie-Peace-Finlay, 2,635 miles (4,241 km)

Largest Lake: Superior, the largest freshwater lake in the world

Canada is the second largest country in the world. Greenland is the largest island in the world.

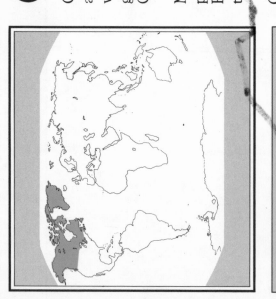

Activities

- In which province is Calgary?
- On which lake is Yellowknife?
- Which two islands lie on the Arctic Circle?
- How far is it from Winnipeg to Montréal?
- What country has authority over Greenland?
- Between which two lakes is Sault Sainte Marie?
- In which direction do you travel from Sudbury to Montréal?
- In which bay do latitude 60° N and longitude 85° W meet?

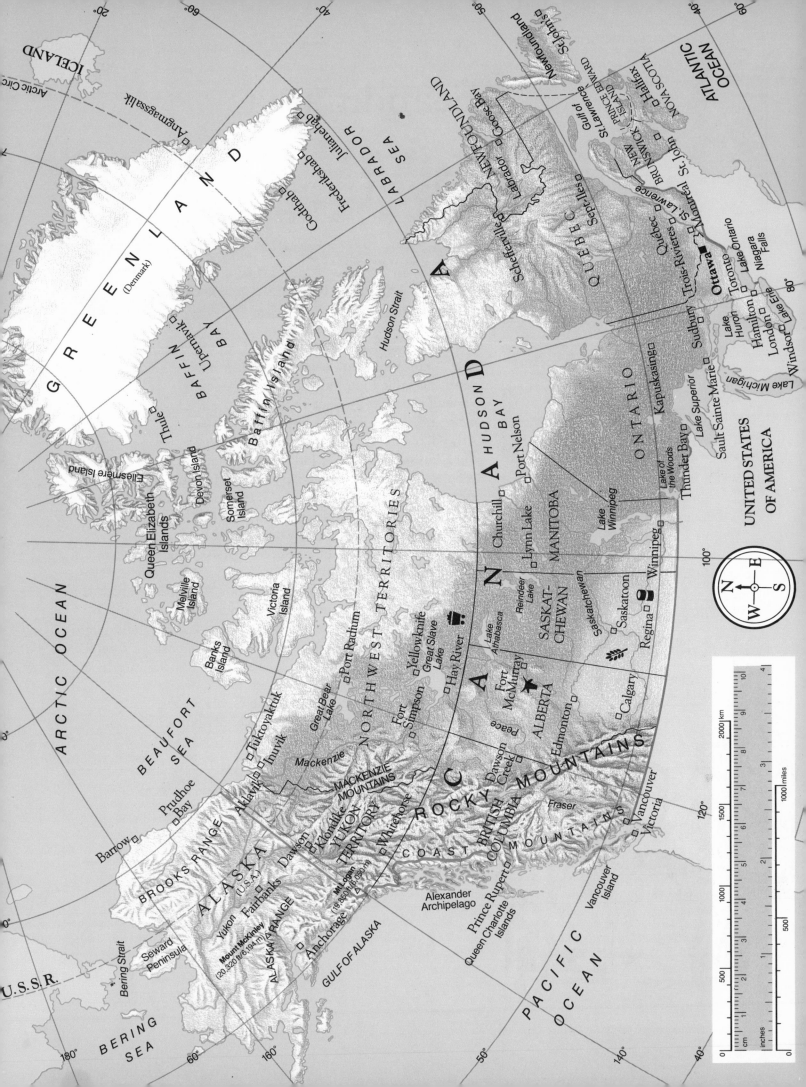

ICELAND

Arctic Circle

Angmagssalik

GREENLAND
(Denmark)

Frederikshåb
Julianehåb

Godthåb

Upernivik

Thule

LABRADOR SEA

BAFFIN BAY

Ellesmere Island

Hudson Strait

NEWFOUNDLAND

Newfoundland

St. John's

Goose Bay

Gulf of St. Lawrence

PRINCE EDWARD ISLAND

NEW BRUNSWICK

NOVA SCOTIA

Halifax

St. John

ATLANTIC OCEAN

QUEBEC

Sept-Îles

Schefferville

Labrador

St. Lawrence

Québec

Trois-Rivières

Montreal

Ottawa

Toronto

Lake Ontario

Niagara Falls

Lake Erie

Windsor

London

Hamilton

Lake Huron

Sudbury

Sault Sainte Marie

Lake Superior

Thunder Bay

Kapuskasing

ONTARIO

Lake of the Woods

Lake Michigan

UNITED STATES OF AMERICA

Queen Elizabeth Islands

Devon Island

Somerset Island

Melville Island

Banks Island

Victoria Island

Baffin Island

ARCTIC OCEAN

BEAUFORT SEA

C A N A D A

HUDSON BAY

Churchill

Port Nelson

Lynn Lake

Reindeer Lake

MANITOBA

Lake Winnipeg

Winnipeg

NORTHWEST TERRITORIES

Port Radium

Great Bear Lake

Yellowknife

Great Slave Lake

Hay River

Lake Athabasca

SASKAT-CHEWAN

Saskatchewan

Saskatoon

Regina

Tuktoyaktuk

Inuvik

Aklavik

Prudhoe Bay

Barrow

Mackenzie

MACKENZIE MOUNTAINS

Fort Simpson

Fort McMurray

Peace

ALBERTA

Edmonton

Calgary

BROOKS RANGE

ALASKA (U.S.A.)

Fairbanks

Dawson

Klondike

YUKON TERRITORY

Whitehorse

COAST

ROCKY MOUNTAINS

Dawson Creek

BRITISH COLUMBIA

MOUNTAINS

Fraser

Vancouver

Victoria

Vancouver Island

Seward Peninsula

Bering Strait

U.S.S.R.

BERING SEA

Yukon

ALASKA RANGE

Mount McKinley
(20,320 ft/6,194 m)

Anchorage

GULF OF ALASKA

Alexander Archipelago

Prince Rupert

Queen Charlotte Islands

PACIFIC OCEAN

Mt Logan
(19,850 ft/6,050 m)

N
W E
S

2000 km

1500

1000

500

1000 miles

500

cm

inches

Scandinavia

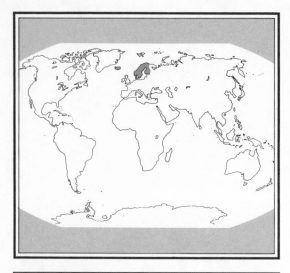

Activities

- Which Scandinavian country is farthest from the Arctic Circle?

- What is the capital of Iceland?

- In which direction do you travel from Malmö to Stockholm?

- Which Swedish town is east of Copenhagen?

- Which gulf separates Sweden and Finland?

- How far is it from Oslo to Copenhagen?

- In which ocean is Iceland?

- Approximately how far is it across Iceland from east to west?

- Which latitude touches the northern tip of Iceland?

- Which Scandinavian country has the northernmost point?

These Samit (Lapps) are herding reindeer.

Denmark, Sweden, Norway, Iceland, and Finland make up the part of Europe called Scandinavia. Denmark is made up of a peninsula called Jutland and about 500 small islands. It has some of the most productive farms in the world and exports meat and cheese to other European countries.

Sweden and Finland are beautiful countries, covered with thick forests. The paper industry in Sweden is important to the people. Huge mills turn wood from the forests into paper. Finland is peppered with lakes. There are about 60,000 in all. Norway is very mountainous, with deep fjords (see above) cut into the coastline by large glaciers in the last Ice Age. Many fishing trawlers leave the coastal towns to gather their catch of fish in the North Sea.

The northern parts of Scandinavia are sometimes called "the land of the midnight Sun." Because the land is so far north, beyond the Arctic Circle, the Sun shines all through the night for a few days each summer. In winter the opposite is true: For a few days, the Sun does not rise above the horizon. In the far north, Samit (Lapps) herd reindeer.

Iceland is just south of the Arctic Circle, in the North Atlantic. As in Norway, fishing is very important to the people who live there. The landscape is frozen and covered in parts by glaciers. Yet Iceland is home to active volcanoes and hot springs that bubble up from under Earth's surface.

Regional Facts

Population: 22.4 million

Largest Country: Sweden

Smallest Country: Denmark

Largest City: Stockholm, Sweden, 1.5 million people

Highest Mountain: Galdhoppigen, Norway, 8,103 ft (2,469 m)

Longest River: Glama, Norway, 380 miles (611 km)

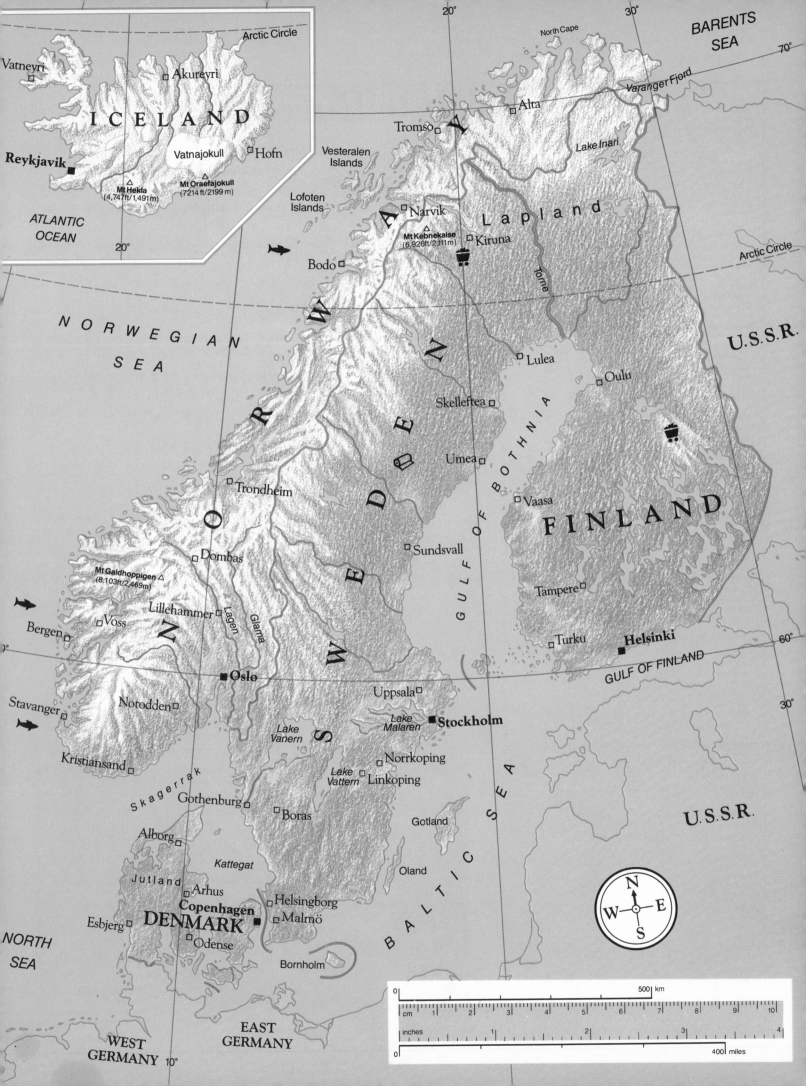

ICELAND

Vatneyri

Akureyri

Reykjavik

Vatnajokull

Hofn

Mt Hekla
(4,747ft/1,491m)

Mt Oraefajokull
(7214 ft/2199 m)

ATLANTIC
OCEAN

20°

Arctic Circle

North Cape

BARENTS
SEA

Alta

Varanger Fjord

70°

Tromso

Lake Inari

Vesteralen
Islands

Lofoten
Islands

Lapland

Narvik

Mt Kebnekaise
(6,926ft/2,111m)

Kiruna

Torne

Bodo

Arctic Circle

NORWEGIAN
SEA

Lulea

U.S.S.R.

Oulu

Skelleftea

GULF OF BOTHNIA

Umea

Vaasa

FINLAND

Trondheim

Dombas

Mt Galdhoppigen
(8,103ft/2,469m)

Sundsvall

Tampere

Lillehammer

Lagen

Glama

Voss

Turku

Helsinki

60°

Bergen

Oslo

GULF OF FINLAND

Stavanger

Notodden

Uppsala

30°

Kristiansand

Lake
Vanern

Lake
Malaren

Stockholm

Norrkoping

Skagerrak

Gothenburg

Lake
Vatten

Linkoping

Boras

Gotland

BALTIC SEA

Alborg

Kattegat

Oland

U.S.S.R.

Jutland

Arhus

Helsingborg

N

Copenhagen

Malmö

W   E

Esbjerg

DENMARK

Odense

S

NORTH
SEA

Bornholm

WEST
GERMANY

EAST
GERMANY

10°

0   500 km

cm   1   2   3   4   5   6   7   8   9   10

inches   1   2   3   4

0   400 miles

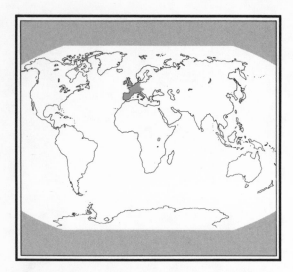

West Europe

Industry is very important to the countries of western Europe. Things made in European factories are sold all over the world. Farming is also a major business in Europe. Grapes and olives are two of the many products grown in the warm countries of the Mediterranean (Italy, France, Portugal, and Spain). Dairy produce and grain are more common in the colder, wetter countries, like Germany and Britain.

France is the largest country in Europe. It has always been popular with vacationers for its varied landscape, warm climate, good food and wine, and beautiful cities.

Switzerland and Austria are mountainous, and many people from other countries are lured to the Alps by winter skiing. The Low Countries consist of Belgium, the Netherlands, and Luxembourg. Some of the land in the Netherlands is below sea level. Great dikes have been built to keep the sea from flooding the fertile land behind them.

Spain and Portugal are also popular with tourists. Portugal is the world's leading producer of cork, which comes from the bark of a tree grown in that country. Spain was ruled by the Romans for over 600 years, and the remains of Roman buildings and walls can be seen all over the country. The Arabs also conquered parts of Spain in the Middle Ages. One of their most famous sites is the Alhambra, a palace near Granada, in southern Spain.

Activities

- Which islands lie to the east of Valencia, Spain?
- What is the longitude of London, England?
- Which three countries border on Luxembourg?
- Which river flows through Paris?
- What is the capital of Portugal?
- In which direction do you travel from Paris to Barcelona?
- Which four countries make up the United Kingdom?
- Which mountain range separates France from Spain?
- How far is it from London to Edinburgh?
- Which sea is to the east of Scotland?

Grape-picking is a common sight in countries like France, Spain, and Italy. Most of the grapes will be used to make wine.

Regional Facts

Population: 320 million

Largest Country: France

Smallest Country: Vatican City

Largest City: London, England, 6.7 million people

Highest Mountain: Mont Blanc, France, 15,771 ft (4,807 m)

Longest River: Rhine, 820 miles (1,320 km)

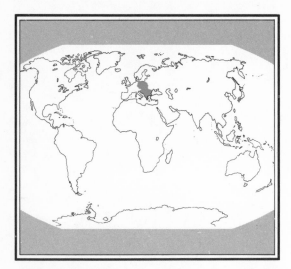

East Europe

The peoples in this part of Europe have many different customs and histories. Ancient Greek civilization and its writers and philosophers have influenced all Europe — and the Western world — with their ideas. Many ancient Greek buildings, like the Parthenon in Athens, still remain.

Yugoslavia and Greece are popular with tourists today because of their warm Mediterranean climate, their beaches, and their beautiful old towns.

Poland is the largest country in this part of Europe. It has big ports on the Baltic Sea and many large industries, and it produces a lot of coal. Czechoslovakia and Hungary do not have a coastline. They use the Danube River to carry large barges laden with goods up and down their countries. The Danube also forms part of the border between Romania and Bulgaria before it finally flows out into the Black Sea. Great cities, like Budapest, have grown up on its banks.

The countryside is a mixture of large, flat plains, where farmers grow crops and keep animals, and mountain ranges with sheltered valleys and winding rivers. Farming is very important to the livelihoods of many of the people.

Activities

- Which two countries are on the eastern edge of the Adriatic Sea?

- What is the capital of Poland?

- Which river flows through Budapest, the capital of Hungary?

- Which Greek island is farthest south?

- How far is it from Warsaw to Athens?

- In which direction do you travel to get from Belgrade to Bucharest?

- Which five countries lie on longitude 20° E?

- Into which sea does the Danube River flow?

Budapest is the capital city of Hungary. It has grown up on both banks of the Danube River.

Regional Facts

Population: 148 million

Largest Country: Poland

Smallest Country: Albania

Largest City: Athens, Greece, 3 million people

Highest Mountain: Olympus, Greece, 9,570 ft (2,917 m)

Longest River: Danube, 1,776 miles (2,858 km)

DENMARK

BALTIC SEA

10°

20°

30°

Rostock

Gdańsk

Szczecin

Oder

Elbe

Berlin

EAST GERMANY

POZNAŃ

Vistula

POLAND

Warsaw

Leipzig

Weimar

Jena

Dresden

Łódź

Wrocław

ORE MOUNTAINS

U.S.S.R.

50°

WEST GERMANY

Prague

CZECHOSLOVAKIA

Ostrava

Kraków

CARPATHIAN MOUNTAINS

Brno

TATRA MOUNTAINS

Košice

Bratislava

AUSTRIA

Danube

Budapest

Miskolc

Debrecen

HUNGARY

Lake Balaton

Cluj

Hungarian Plain

Pécs

Szeged

ROMANIA

Zagreb

Arad

Mureș

Mt Moldoveanul
(8,348ft/2,548m)

Brașov

Rijeka

Timișoara

TRANSYLVANIAN ALPS

Ploiești

Drava

Sava

Belgrade

Bucharest

YUGOSLAVIA

Constanța

BLACK SEA

DINARIC ALPS

Sarajevo

Danube

BALKAN MOUNTAINS

BULGARIA

Varna

ITALY

Split

Dalmatia

ADRIATIC SEA

Dubrovnik

Skopje

Sofia

Stara Zagora

Burgas

Plovdiv

Tirana

ALBANIA

Vlorë

Korçë

Thessaloniki

Corfu

Mt Olympus
(9,570 ft/2,918 m)

40°

Ionian Islands

PINDUS MOUNTAINS

AEGEAN SEA

Lesbos

TURKEY

GREECE

Chios

Patrai

Athens

Corinth

Peloponnese

MEDITERRANEAN SEA

N
W   E
S

Rhodes

Crete

30°

500 km

cm 1 2 3 4 5 6 7 8 9 10

inches 1 2 3 4

500 miles

Northern Africa

The boundaries of the vast Sahara Desert are unclear, but it is nearly as big as the U.S. and stretches across almost all of northern Africa, covering part or all of at least ten countries. Scattered across the desert are oases, where water is found. Many oases are single small springs with a few palm trees. Nomads who live in the desert bring their animals to drink there.

In the northern part of the Sahara, most people speak Arabic. In Egypt, people live along the fertile Nile Valley. The Nile is the longest river in the world, flowing all the way from central Africa to the Mediterranean Sea. Before the Aswan High Dam was completed in 1971, the Nile flooded once a year. The rich soil left by the river on both of its banks is very fertile. This has helped farmers since the time of the ancient Egyptians, who built the Pyramids and Sphinx.

The Blue Nile begins in Ethiopia, one of the poorest countries in the world. Despite large amounts of foreign aid, the people have suffered widespread famine. Across the continent, in Nigeria, the situation is somewhat different. The discovery of oil has brought wealth to that country, but Nigeria still has economic problems. Most African nations were once European colonies, but today they are independent nations. Whether they are relatively rich or poor depends a lot on their natural resources and climate.

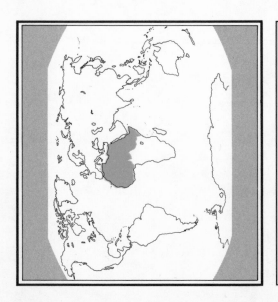

The Aswan High Dam, on the Nile River in Egypt.

Regional Facts

Population: 293 million

Largest Country: The Sudan

Smallest Country: São Tomé and Principe (see page 29)

Largest City: Cairo, Egypt, 5 million people

Highest Mountain: Ras Dashan, Ethiopia, 15,157 ft (4,620 m)

Longest River: Nile, 4,132 miles (6,650 km) — longest river in the world

Activities

• How far is it from Algiers to Lagos?

• In which direction do you travel to get from Algiers to Lagos?

• Which four countries border on Lake Chad?

• Is the White Nile west or east of the Blue Nile?

• What is the longitude of Lake Volta, Ghana?

• What is the capital of Ethiopia?

• What is the highest point in the Atlas Mountains, Morocco?

• Which seas are connected by the Suez Canal?

• What is the quickest route by sea from Mogadiscio, Somalia, to Italy?

• Name the countries on the coast between Guinea and Nigeria.

40° 30° 20° 10° 0° 50°

ATLANTIC OCEAN

SPAIN

ITALY

GREECE

TURKEY

MEDITERRANEAN SEA

Tangier
Casablanca
Rabat
MOROCCO
Marrakech
Mt Toubkal △
(13,665 ft/4,165 m)
ATLAS MOUNTAINS
Fes
Meknes
Oran
Mostaganem
Algiers
Annaba
Constantine
Tunis
TUNISIA
Sfax
Tripoli
Misratah
Benghazi
Al Bayda
Ajdabiyah
Alexandria
Tanta
Mahalla el Kubra
Port Said
Suez Canal
ISRAEL
Cairo
Giza
El Minya
Asyut

SAUDI ARABIA

RED SEA

Port Sudan

Aswan
Lake Nasser

EGYPT

Libyan Desert

LIBYA

Sebha
Ubari

SAHARA DESERT

TIBESTI MOUNTAINS

Tindouf
Bechar
In Salah
Reggane
HOGGAR MOUNTAINS
△ Mt Tahat
(9,852 ft/3,003 m)
Tamanrasset

ALGERIA

F'Derik
Atar
El Aaiun
WESTERN SAHARA
Canary Islands (Spain)
Tropic of Cancer

MAURITANIA

Nouakchott

Dakar
SENEGAL
Banjul
THE GAMBIA
GUINEA-BISSAU
Bissau
Conakry
GUINEA
Kankan
SIERRA LEONE
Freetown
Monrovia
LIBERIA
Mt Nimba
(5,748 ft/1,752 m)

Senegal

MALI

Bamako
BURKINA FASO
Ouagadougou
Tombouctou
Gao

Niger

NIGER

Niamey

Kumasi
Accra
Abidjan
IVORY COAST
Bouake
GHANA
Lake Volta
TOGO
BENIN
Lome
Cotonou
Porto Novo
GULF OF GUINEA

NIGERIA
Kano
Jos
Abuja
Ilorin
Ogbomosho
Ibadan
Lagos
Onitsha
Port Harcourt
Benue
Maiduguri

CHAD

N'Djamena

Lake Chad

Chari

CENTRAL AFRICAN REPUBLIC

ZAIRE

SUDAN

Omdurman
Khartoum
El Obeid
El Fasher
Wad Medani
Kassala

Blue Nile
White Nile
Nile
Atbara

The Sudd
Juba

UGANDA

KENYA

Eritrea
Asmara
Mt Ras Dashan △
(15,157 ft/4,620 m)
Lake Tana
Addis Ababa
ETHIOPIA
Jimma
Diredawa
DJIBOUTI
Djibouti
Berbera
Ogaden

SOMALIA

Mogadiscio
Kismayu

INDIAN OCEAN

Equator

N E S W (compass)

0 500 1000 1500 2000 km
0 500 1000 1500 miles
cm 1 2 3 4 5 6 7 8 9 10
inches 1 2 3 4

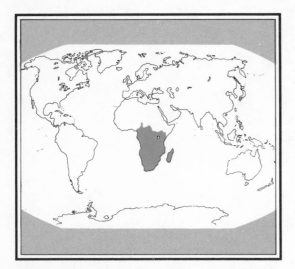

Central and Southern Africa

Countries like Kenya and Tanzania are famous for their wildlife parks.

Activities

- Which African country is farthest south?
- Approximately how long is Lake Malawi?
- Which two countries share the Victoria Falls?
- In which direction do you travel from Malawi to Congo?
- How far is it between the peaks of Mount Kenya and Mount Kilimanjaro?
- What is the other, older name for the Zaire River?
- Which cape would you sail around to get from Madagascar to Namibia?
- In which countries is the Kalahari Desert?
- Which six African countries lie on the Equator?

Regional Facts

Population: 176 million

Largest Country: Zaire

Smallest Country: Seychelles (islands; not on map)

Largest City: Johannesburg, South Africa, 1.4 million people

Highest Mountain: Kilimanjaro, Tanzania, 19,340 ft (5,895 m)

Longest River: Zaire, 2,718 miles (4,374 km)

Largest Lake: Victoria — the second largest freshwater lake in the world

Much of central Africa is covered by savanna, flat grassland with patches of trees and scrub. This is the home of the last great herds of wild animals — lions, giraffes, zebras, elephants, and many others. The nations of eastern Africa, such as Kenya and Tanzania, are famous for their wildlife. People can go on safari and see animals roaming in the wild.

At the heart of southern Africa is the Kalahari Desert, where native tribes still live in their traditional way. Often, women collect nuts and berries to eat, and men hunt animals with bows and poisoned arrows.

There are many different black African peoples, from the smallest people in the world, the Pygmies of the rain forests, to the tall Masai of the savanna. Many whites of European descent live in the Republic of South Africa. Though most people living there are black, whites govern this country under apartheid, a cruel system that keeps nonwhites from enjoying the same rights as whites have. Most black Africans in South Africa are from four major groups: the Nguni, the Sotho, the San, and the Khoikhoi.

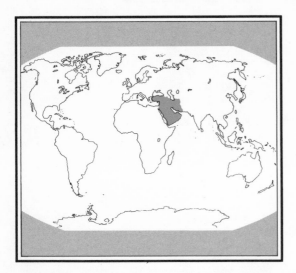

Southwest Asia

This region, which is part of the Middle East, is sometimes called "the cradle of civilization." Some of the most ancient civilizations were born here, as well as three major religions — Judaism, Christianity, and Islam. This region is also where three continents — Europe, Asia, and Africa — meet.

Most people here are Arabs, and their language is primarily Arabic. Turkey and Iran are non-Arabic nations, but like the Arabs, most people there are Muslims. Muslims believe that there is one God (Allah) and that his Prophet is Muhammad. There are Christians in Cyprus and Christians and Muslims in Israel, where most people are Jewish, and in Lebanon. The ancient Holy Land of Palestine (where Israel and Jordan are today) is sacred to Jews, Muslims, and Christians. Today, the Middle East is a scene of powerful political and religious turmoil.

Much of the Middle East is desert. It is very hot during the day and cold at night. The discovery of oil has made countries like Saudi Arabia, Bahrain, Qatar, Kuwait, and Iran wealthy. Tankers transport oil from the Persian Gulf to Europe through the Red Sea and Suez Canal.

Activities

- Which country forms the northeastern coast of the Persian Gulf?

- In which direction do you sail from Aden, Yemen, to the island of Socotra?

- Which country is north of Syria?

- What is the capital of Jordan?

- What two countries are separated by the Straits of Hormuz?

- In which country is the holy city of Mecca?

- How far is it from Mecca to Jerusalem?

- What is the longitude of Aden, Yemen?

- Which sea is close to the Elburz Mountains?

- Which Mediterranean island is in the Middle East?

Regional Facts

Population: 135 million

Largest Country: Saudi Arabia

Smallest Country: Bahrain

Largest City: Tehran, Iran, 4.5 million people

Highest Mountain: Damavand, Iran, 18,376 ft (5,601 m)

Longest River: Euphrates, 1,700 miles (2,736 km)

Oil tankers travel through the Red Sea and Suez Canal with their cargo of oil.

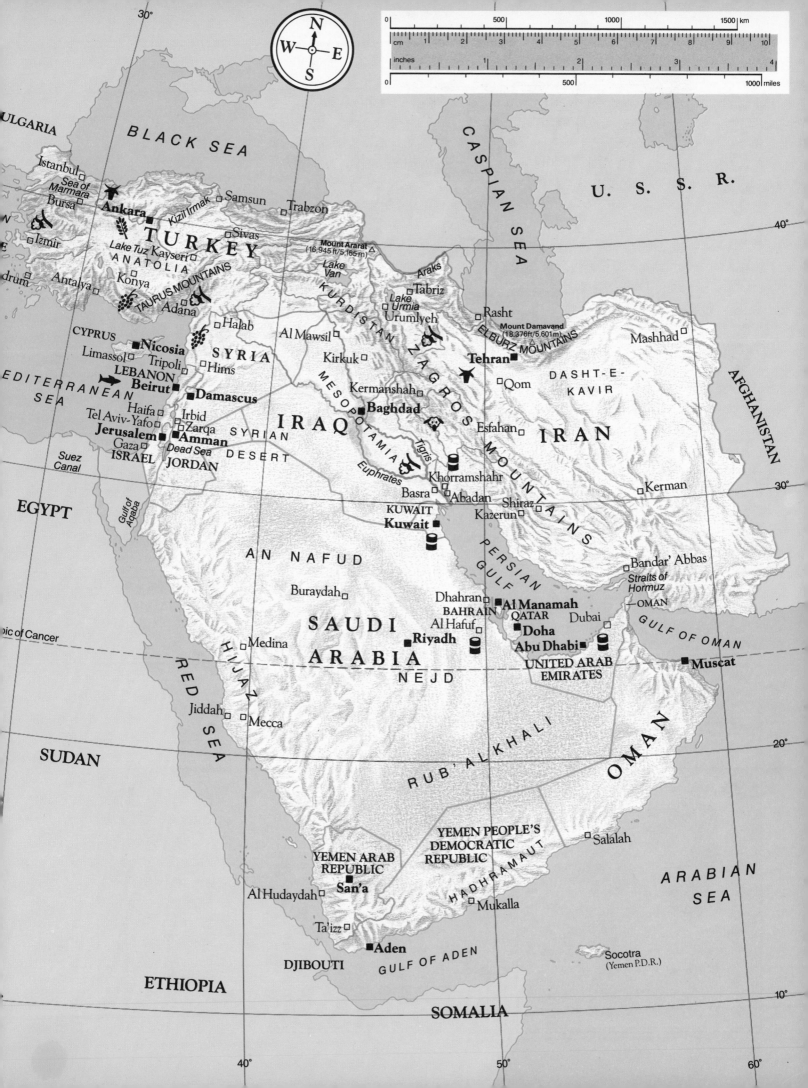

Union of Soviet Socialist Republics

The U.S.S.R. (Soviet Union) is the largest nation in the world. It is made up of fifteen states called republics. The biggest republic is the Russian Soviet Federated Socialist Republic, with over half the population of the entire country. That is why the U.S.S.R. is often called Russia. More than sixty languages are used throughout the country, but Russian is the only language spoken everywhere.

Soviets are district councils, and the country is run through these by a system of government control and ownership called communism. Property is owned by the community, and each citizen is expected to work for the benefit of the community according to his or her abilities. A quarter of the Soviet Union is farmland, and many farmers work on enormous state-owned farms. Others work on small collectives, sharing profits with each other and the state. The Soviet Union is the world's top producer of barley, potatoes, wheat, milk, and butter.

The U.S.S.R. is also a powerful industrial nation. It has vast resources of coal, oil, and natural gas, and is the world's leading producer of steel and petroleum.

The U.S.S.R. has great military strength. With the United States and China, it is one of the world's three biggest superpowers. It also has an extensive space program. Both the first man and the first woman in space were Soviets.

Country Facts

Population: 262.5 million

Capital City: Moscow

Largest City: Moscow, 8 million people

Highest Mountain: Pik Kommunizma, 24,590 ft (7,495 m)

Longest River: Ob-Irtysh, 3,362 miles (5,411 km)

The Soviet Union is the largest country in the world.

Activities

- On which sea is Baku?
- Can you find the Black Sea and the White Sea?
- How far is it from Odessa to Leningrad?
- How many degrees of longitude does the Soviet Union extend from west to east?
- In which direction do you travel to get from Moscow to Leningrad?
- Between which two seas are the Caucasus Mountains?
- Which city is farthest west — Kiev, Moscow, or Leningrad?
- Which ocean is to the north of the Soviet Union?
- Is the U.S.S.R. twice as big as China?
- Which plateau is above the Arctic Circle?

(Above right) The U.S.S.R. has an extensive space program.

India and its neighbors

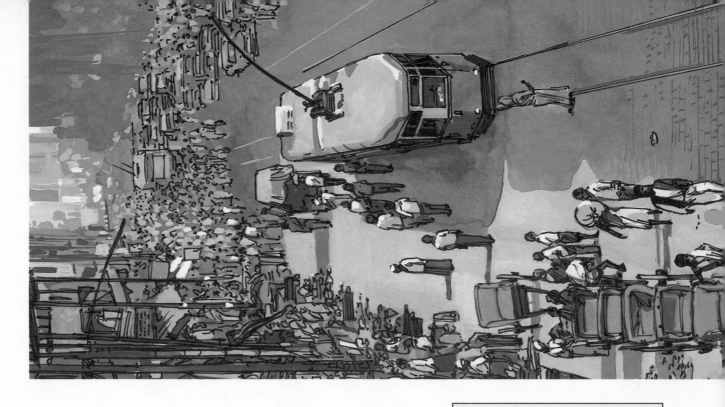

This part of the world is one of great contrasts in scenery. Northern India, Afghanistan, Bhutan, Pakistan, and Nepal are very mountainous. The highest mountain range in the world, the Himalayas, forms a spectacular border between Tibetan China and Nepal and Bhutan.

India, Pakistan, and Bangladesh are densely populated countries. India alone has 684 million people. Most live in villages and work on the land growing food. It is difficult for these nations to grow enough to feed all their people.

Most of the rain needed to grow crops falls in just a few weeks of the year. This is called the monsoon. Too much rain means floods; too little, and there will be drought.

Many different religious groups inhabit this region. Among them are Hindus, Muslims (especially in Pakistan and Bangladesh), Parsis (in Bombay), Christians, Sikhs, Buddhists, and many others.

Regional Facts

Population: 933 million

Largest Country: India

Smallest Country: Maldives

Largest City: Calcutta, India, 7 million people

Highest Mountain: Everest, Nepal/Tibetan China, 29,028 ft (8,848 m) — the highest mountain in the world

Longest River: Indus, 1,800 miles (2,900 km)

India has many large and crowded cities. This is Calcutta, in northeast India.

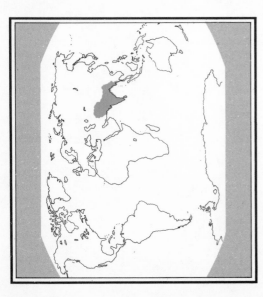

Activities

- What is the capital of Sri Lanka?
- Into which bay does the Ganges River flow?
- The second highest mountain in the world is in Pakistan, near the Indian border. What is it called?
- How far is it from Bombay to Calcutta?
- Which country is west of the Thar Desert, India?
- In which sea is the position 25° N, 65° E?
- Which country stretches farther south, Bangladesh or Pakistan?
- In which country is Kathmandu?
- To which country do the Andaman Islands belong?

China, Japan, and their neighbors

The Great Wall of China.

China is the world's third largest country. It is also the world's most populated country. A main part of the people's diet is rice, which is grown in flooded fields in southern and central China. In the cooler, drier areas of the north and east, farmers grow wheat and corn. China is the world's top producer of cotton and tobacco. While most people work as farmers, today many people in the cities work in modern factories.

Over its long history, China has often been closed to outsiders. Today, tourists visit the Great Wall, which dates back some 2,200 years and is about 1,500 miles (2,400 km) long.

Japan is the richest country in Asia. It has many successful industries that sell their products all over the world. Since World War II, Japan has become a world leader in producing calculators, cars, typewriters, pianos, and ships.

Japan is made up of four big islands (Hokkaido, Honshu, Shikoku, and Kyushu) and about 3,000 smaller ones. About fifty of Japan's mountains are active volcanoes. Fujiyama is the highest.

Regional Facts

Population: 1.15 billion

Largest Country: China — the third largest in the world

Smallest Country: Taiwan

Largest City: Tokyo, Japan, 11 million people

Highest Mountain: Everest, Tibetan China/Nepal, 29,028 ft (8,848 m) — the highest mountain in the world

Longest River: Chang Jiang, 3,964 miles (6,380 km) — the third longest river in the world

Fujiyama, a volcano, is the highest point in Japan.

Activities

- Which two countries in the world are larger than China?

- Into which sea does the Chang Jiang river flow?

- In which direction is Japan from Hong Kong?

- What is Japan's highest mountain?

- To which country does Hong Kong currently belong?

- How far is it from Shanghai to Hong Kong?

- What is the large desert in southern Mongolia and northern China called?

- What is the Chinese name for the city long called Peking?

- What is the capital of South Korea?

- Which of Japan's four large islands is farthest north?

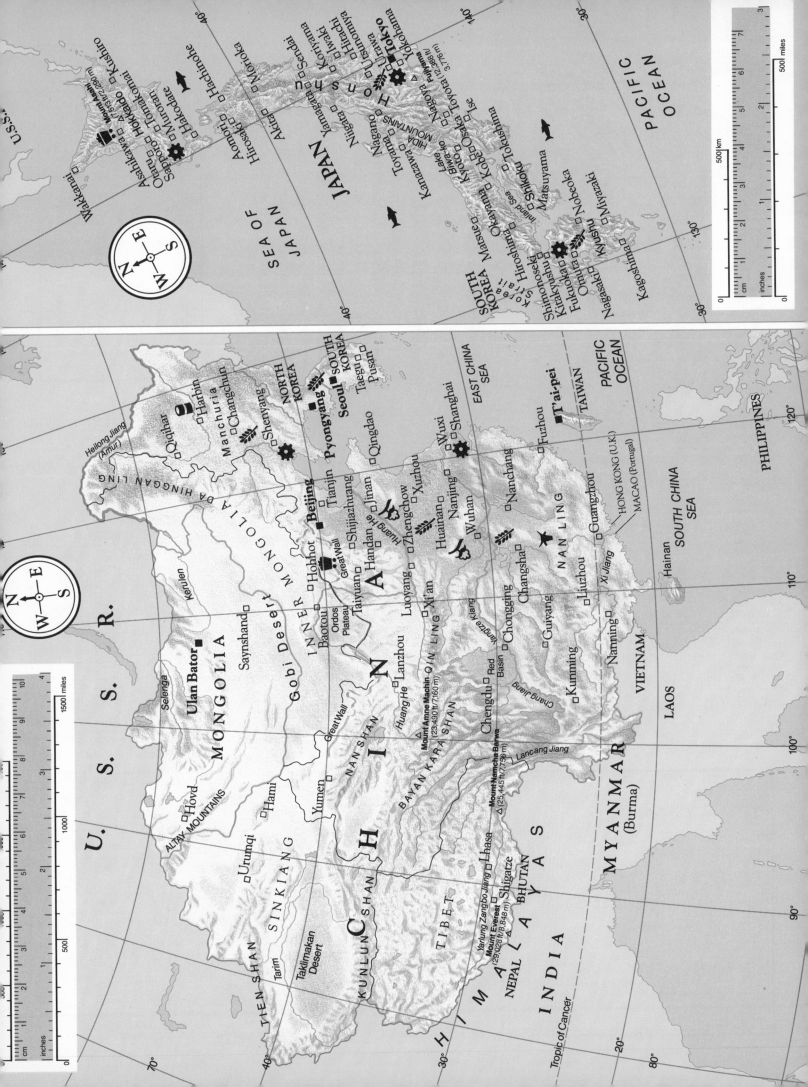

Southeast Asia

People at work on terraced rice fields.

Much of Southeast Asia is made up of islands. Indonesia has over 13,000 islands, and the Philippines has more than 7,000. Many are volcanic. This region is hot and wet all year round. For a few months each year there is a heavy rain season, called the monsoon.

Many people live in Southeast Asia. The cities are overcrowded, with poor people living on the city edges in shanty towns. Their homes are made of scrap wood and corrugated iron. Most people live on low land near the coasts and in river valleys. Many farm the land, growing rice, vegetables, spices, and fruit. Rice is a major food in this region. It is often grown on flat terraces on the sides of hills and mountains.

The many mountains are covered with thick rain forests. Some of the wood from the trees, such as teak and mahogany, is valuable. Some trees provide useful materials other than wood. The sap from the rubber tree, for example, gives us rubber. Malaysia, Indonesia, and Thailand are the world's top rubber producers. Malaysia alone produces over half the world's natural rubber. It also produces one-third of the world's tin.

Vietnam, Laos, and Kampuchea (Cambodia) are poor countries. They have suffered greatly in recent years from war and political changes.

Music, dance, plays, and handmade crafts keep alive the ancient legends of Southeast Asia. Most of the people are Buddhists or Muslims. Temple dancers tell the stories of their religion as they dance.

Regional Facts

Population: 320 million
Largest Country: Indonesia
Smallest Country: Singapore
Largest City: Jakarta, Indonesia, 6.5 million people
Highest Mountain: Jaya, Indonesia, 16,502 ft (5,030 m)
Longest River: Mekong, 2,610 miles (4,200 km)

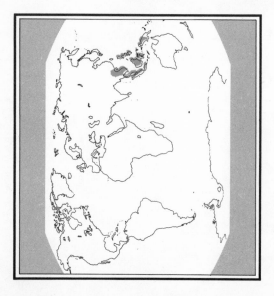

Activities

- How far is it across the South China Sea from Da Nang to Manila?

- In which direction do you travel from Ho Chi Minh to Hanoi?

- What is the capital of Thailand?

- Two large and two small major Southeast Asian islands are on the Equator. Which are they?

- In which ocean are the Philippines?

- Which strait divides Malaysia from Sumatra?

- Is Bali east, west, north, or south of Java?

- Into which sea does the Mekong River flow?

- Which three countries border on Kampuchea (Cambodia)?

- To which group of islands does Halmahera belong?

CHINA

Hanoi
Haiphong
Gulf of Tonkin
Luang Prabang
Hong
LAOS
Chiang Mai
Vientiane
THAILAND
Mekong
Nakhon Ratchasima
Ubon Ratchathani
Bangkok
KAMPUCHEA
(CAMBODIA)
Thon Buri
Lake Tonle Sap
Phnom Penh
VIETNAM
Hue
Da Nang
Qui Nhon
Nha Trang
Ho Chi Minh
Gulf of Thailand
Surat Thani
Isthmus of Kra
ANDAMAN SEA

SOUTH CHINA SEA

Banda Aceh
Medan
Kota Baharu
PENINSULAR
MALAYSIA
MALAYSIA
Pinang
Ipoh
Kuala Lumpur
Malacca
Johor Baharu
SINGAPORE
Strait of Malacca
Sumatra
Padang
Mentawai Islands
INDIAN OCEAN

Jambi
Palembang
Bangka
Greater Sunda Islands
Jakarta
Bandung
Yogjakarta
Java
Malang
Surabaya

PACIFIC OCEAN

PHILIPPINES
Luzon
Manila
Quezon City
Mindoro
Samar
Panay
Iloilo
Cebu
Negros
Leyte
Butuan
Mindanao
Davao
General Santos
Zamboanga
Sulu Archipelago
SULU SEA
Palawan

Mount Kinabalu
(13,455 ft/4,101 m)
SABAH
Bandar Seri Begawan
BRUNEI
SARAWAK
Kuching
Borneo
KALIMANTAN
Samarinda

CELEBES SEA
Manado
Sulawesi
Ujung Pandang
Strait of Makassar

Molucca Islands
Ternate
Halmahera
Buru
Seram
Ambon
BANDA SEA

Equator

New Guinea
IRIAN JAYA
MAOKE MOUNTAINS
Java Peak (16,502 ft/5,030 m)
Kolepom Island
Aru Islands
Tanimbar Islands
ARAFURA SEA

INDONESIA
N
D
O
N
E
S
I
A

JAVA SEA
Bali
Lombok
Singaradja
Sumbawa
Lesser Sunda Islands
Sumbawa
Ende
Flores
FLORES SEA
Sumba
Kupang
Timor
TIMOR SEA

AUSTRALIA

N
W E
S

0°
10°
20°
100°
110°
120°
130°
140°
10°

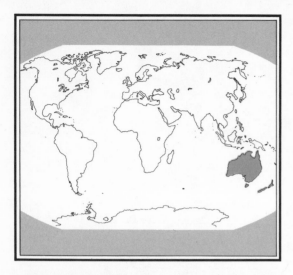

Australia and New Zealand

Australia is a country of contrasts. It has a small population, yet most of its people live in crowded cities and towns. It is the smallest continent with the greatest proportion of desert, yet one of the richest nations. It is one of the oldest land masses on Earth, yet one of the last to be developed by people. Perhaps the greatest contrast is between the Outback of vast, flat desert and sheep and cattle stations and the coastal cities where most Australians live and work. Australia also claims the distinction of being the top wool producer in the world and has many more sheep than people.

The first Australians were the Aboriginals. They have been living there for at least 40,000 years. About 200 years ago, people came from many countries in Europe, especially from Britain, and settled in what was to them a new country. They brought lifestyles with them that were quite different from the Aboriginal way of life. Major cities, like Melbourne and Sydney, look much like the cities of Europe.

The country has a varied climate. The deserts in the center are hot and dry, and the jungles in the north are hot and steamy. On the island of Tasmania, in the south, the temperature is often cool and there is plenty of rain.

The original inhabitants of New Zealand were the Maoris. They came from the Polynesian Islands, and their customs and traditions play an important role in New Zealand today. In the eighteenth and nineteenth centuries people came from Britain to start a new life farming and trading. Today, New Zealand is a rich farming country. Cattle are kept on dairy farms on North Island, and sheep graze on both islands.

Activities

- In which sea is the Great Barrier Reef?

- Which town is right in the middle of Australia?

- Which is the highest mountain in New Zealand?

- How far is it from Perth to Brisbane?

- In which direction do you travel from Sydney to Melbourne?

- In which Australian state is Brisbane?

Regional Facts

Population: Australia, 15.8 million
New Zealand, 3.3 million

Capitals: Australia, Canberra
New Zealand, Wellington

Largest City: Sydney, Australia, 3.2 million people

Highest Mountain: Mount Cook, New Zealand, 12,346 ft (3,764 m)

Longest River: Murray-Darling, Australia, 2,310 miles (3,718 m)

There are more sheep than people in Australia. They provide wool and meat.

INDONESIA

PAPUA NEW GUINEA

ARAFURA SEA

TIMOR SEA

Torres Strait

Melville
Island

INDIAN

OCEAN

Darwin

Arnhem Land

*GULF OF
CARPENTARIA*

Cape York
Peninsula

CORAL SEA

Wyndham

Kimberley
Plateau

Cairns

Townsville

Broome

NORTHERN

TERRITORY

Port Hedland

Dampier

Great Sandy
Desert

Macdonnell
Range

Alice Springs

QUEENSLAND

Rockhampton

Hamersley
Range

Gibson
Desert

Tropic of Capricorn

AUSTRALIA

Cooper Creek

Carnarvon

Ayers Rock

Simpson
Desert

Charleville

Toowoomba

Brisbane

WESTERN

Musgrave Range

Meekatharra

Great Victoria Desert

SOUTH

Lake Eyre

AUSTRALIA

AUSTRALIA

Geraldton

Lake Torrens

NEW SOUTH

Kalgoorlie

Nullarbor Plain

Lake Gairdner

Broken
Hill

WALES

Perth

Fremantle

Esperance

Port Augusta

Port Lincoln

GREAT AUSTRALIAN BIGHT

Adelaide

Darling

Murray

Wagga
Wagga

Sydney

Wollongong

Albany

Canberra
(Australian Capital Territory)

Bendigo

VICTORIA

Mount Kosciusko
(7,316 ft/2,230 m)

Ballarat

Melbourne

*TASMAN
SEA*

Bass Strait

TASMANIA

Launceston

Hobart

---

*PACIFIC
OCEAN*

Auckland

Hamilton

**NEW
ZEALAND**

North Island

Egmont
(8,252 ft/2,516 m)

Wanganui

Napier

Palmerston North

Nelson

Wellington

Greymouth

South Island

Mount Cook
(12,346 ft/3,764 m)

Christchurch

Timaru

SOUTHERN ALPS

Dunedin

Invercargill

N
W E
S

0	500	1000	1500	km

| cm | 1 | 2 | 3 | 4 | 5 | 6 | 7 | 8 | 9 | 10 |

| inches | 1 | 2 | 3 | 4 |

| 0 | 500 | 1000 | miles |

Hawaii (U.S.) and the Pacific islands

Fishing is an important economic activity — and a way of life — on many of the Pacific islands. People still use canoes to venture out to sea to find fish.

Activities

- What is the capital of Tuvalu?

- To which country does Pitcairn Island belong?

- Which continent is to the east of the Galápagos Islands?

- What imaginary line from west to east divides the Pacific Ocean in two?

- Which two countries are separated by the Tasman Sea?

- Which country controls the Trust Territory of the Pacific Islands?

- What is the capital of Fiji?

- Which is the largest ocean on Earth?

Regional Facts

Population: 6 million

Largest Country: Papua New Guinea

Smallest Country: Nauru

Highest Mountain: Mt. Wilhelm, Papua New Guinea (not on map), 15,400 ft (4,694 m)

There are thousands of small islands in the Pacific Ocean. The ocean itself covers almost a third of the Earth's surface. The Pacific Islands fall into three main groups, according to their location and the type of people who live on them. The people of Melanesia tend to be much like the native peoples of Africa and Australia. Native Hawaiians and other people of Polynesia are related to Asian peoples. The people of Micronesia represent a mixture of the other two peoples.

Some of the islands are made of coral, the limestone skeletons of tiny sea animals. Many of these islands are quite mountainous and were created by volcanoes. The major islands of Hawaii are volcanic.

Hawaii, Fiji, and other island groups are popular with tourists, but many of the smaller islands get few visitors. Life on these islands is often simple. People live in small villages, grow food in gardens, and fish from canoes. On larger islands, people work in places like banana or pineapple plantations or mine copper and other minerals.

Some groups of islands are still colonies and belong to other countries. Others are independent, with their own governments. Hawaii became one of the fifty states of the U.S. in 1959.

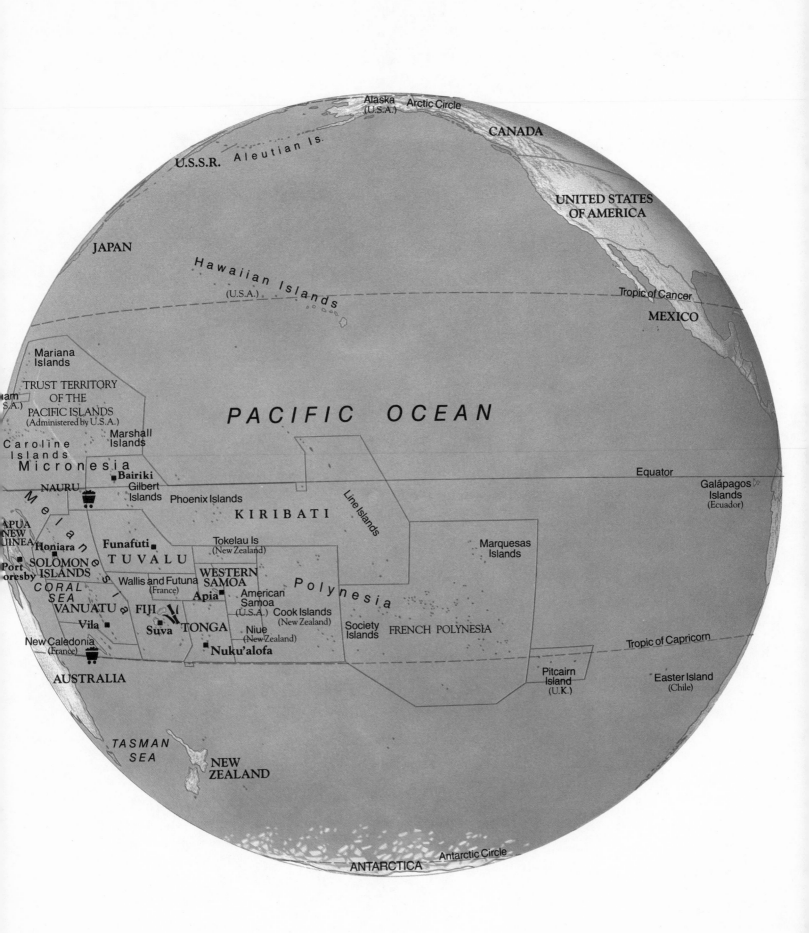

Alaska (U.S.A.) Arctic Circle

CANADA

U.S.S.R. Aleutian Is.

JAPAN

UNITED STATES OF AMERICA

Hawaiian Islands (U.S.A.)

Tropic of Cancer

MEXICO

PACIFIC OCEAN

Mariana Islands

am S.A.)

TRUST TERRITORY OF THE PACIFIC ISLANDS (Administered by U.S.A.)

Marshall Islands

Caroline Islands

Micronesia

Bairiki

NAURU

Gilbert Islands

Equator

Galápagos Islands (Ecuador)

Phoenix Islands

Melanesia

KIRIBATI

Line Islands

APUA NEW UINEA

Honiara

Funafuti

TUVALU

Tokelau Is (New Zealand)

Marquesas Islands

Port oresby

SOLOMON ISLANDS

Wallis and Futuna (France)

WESTERN SAMOA

Polynesia

CORAL SEA

Melanesia

VANUATU

FIJI

Apia

American Samoa (U.S.A.)

Cook Islands (New Zealand)

FRENCH POLYNESIA

Vila

Suva

TONGA

Niue (New Zealand)

Society Islands

New Caledonia (France)

Nuku'alofa

Tropic of Capricorn

Pitcairn Island (U.K.)

Easter Island (Chile)

AUSTRALIA

TASMAN SEA

NEW ZEALAND

Antarctic Circle

ANTARCTICA

150°

180°

150°

PACIFIC
OCEAN

Aleutian Is.

BERING SEA

Bering Strait

ALASKA
(U.S.A.)

Yukon

Barrow

Wrangel
Island

EAST
SIBERIA
SEA

S
I
B
E
R
I
A

Prudhoe Bay

BEAUFORT
SEA

120°

Mackenzie

Inuvik

Tiksi

Lena

New Siberian
Islands

CANADA

Banks
Island

LAPTEV
SEA

U.S.S.R.

ARCTIC OCEAN

Victoria
Island

LOMONOSOV RIDGE

Severnaya
Zemlya

Noril'sk

Ellesmere Island

North Pole

Yenisei

Baffin Island

Thule

Franz Josef
Land
(U.S.S.R.)

KARA SEA

Novaya Zemlya

90°

BAFFIN BAY

Svalbard
(Norway)

Davis Strait

BARENTS
SEA

GREENLAND
(Denmark)

GREENLAND SEA

Murmansk

NORWEGIAN
SEA

NORWAY

Narvik

Arkhangel'sk

Denmark Strait

Arctic Circle

FINLAND

SWEDEN

ATLANTIC
OCEAN

ICELAND

0°

30°

| 0 | 500 | 1000 | 1500 | 2000 km |

| cm | 1 | 2 | 3 | 4 | 5 | 6 | 7 |

| inches | | 1 | | 2 | | 3 |

| 0 | 500 | 1000 | 1500 miles |

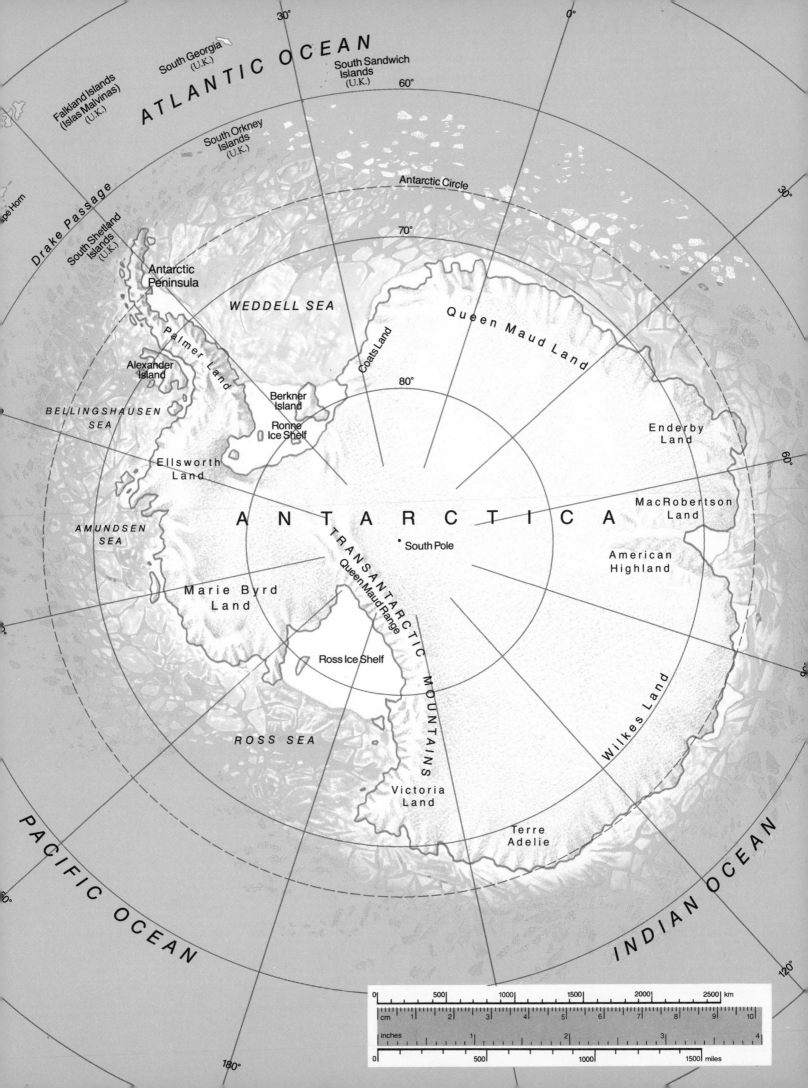

ATLANTIC OCEAN

South Georgia
(U.K.)

Falkland Islands
(Islas Malvinas)
(U.K.)

South Sandwich
Islands
(U.K.)

30°

60°

0°

Cape Horn

Drake Passage

South Orkney
Islands
(U.K.)

Antarctic Circle

South Shetland
Islands (U.K.)

70°

30°

Antarctic
Peninsula

WEDDELL SEA

Queen Maud Land

Palmer Land

Coats Land

Alexander
Island

Berkner
Island

80°

Enderby
Land

BELLINGSHAUSEN
SEA

Ronne
Ice Shelf

Ellsworth
Land

60°

A N T A R C T I C A

MacRobertson
Land

AMUNDSEN
SEA

• South Pole

American
Highland

Marie Byrd
Land

TRANSANTARCTIC MOUNTAINS

Queen Maud Range

Ross Ice Shelf

Wilkes Land

90°

ROSS SEA

Victoria
Land

PACIFIC OCEAN

Terre
Adelie

INDIAN OCEAN

60°

180°

120°

					500		1000		1500		2000		2500 km

cm	1	2	3	4	5	6	7	8	9	10

inches		1		2		3		4

0		500		1000		1500 miles

Map Index

46